This diary belongs to

....

First published in 2018
by Faber & Faber Ltd
Bloomsbury House
74–77 Great Russell Street
London WC1B 3DA

Designed and typeset by Faber & Faber Ltd
Printed in China by Imago

Design by Faber
This book is covered in Liberty London Fabrics' Peacock Parade fabric.
Copyright © Liberty Fabric Limited 2018.

Clauses in the Banking and Financial Dealings Act allow the government
to alter dates at short notice

A CIP record for this book is available from the British Library

ISBN 978–0–571–34169–6

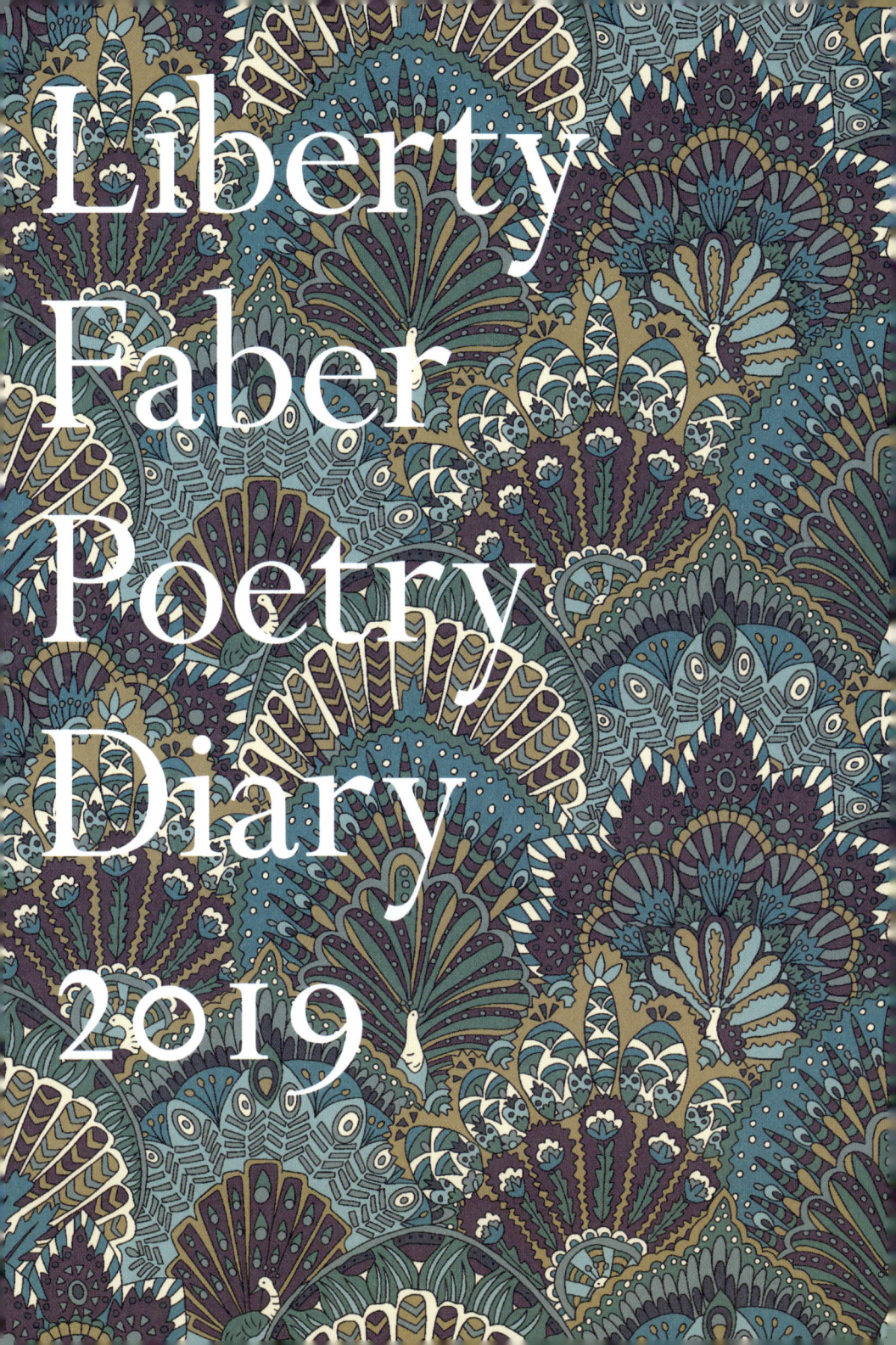

Liberty Faber Poetry Diary 2019

Faber & Faber was founded in 1929 ...

... but its roots go back further to the Scientific Press, which started publishing in the early years of the century. The press's largest shareholders were Sir Maurice and Lady Gwyer, and their desire to expand into general publishing led them to Geoffrey Faber, a fellow of All Souls College, Oxford. Faber and Gwyer was founded in 1925. After four years Faber took the company forward alone, and the story goes that Walter de la Mare suggested adding a second, fictitious Faber to balance the company name.

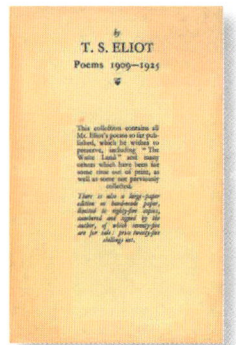

In the meantime, the firm had prospered. T. S. Eliot, who had been suggested to Geoffrey Faber by a colleague at All Souls, had left Lloyds Bank in London to join him as a director, and in its first season the firm issued Eliot's *Poems 1909–1925*. In addition, the catalogues from the early years included books by Jean Cocteau, Herbert Read and Vita Sackville-West.

Poetry was always to be a significant element in the list and under Eliot's aegis Marianne Moore, Louis MacNeice and David Jones soon joined Ezra Pound, W. H. Auden, Stephen Spender, James Joyce, Siegfried Sassoon, D. H. Lawrence and Walter de la Mare.

Under Geoffrey Faber's chairmanship the board in 1929 included Eliot, Richard de la Mare, Charles Stewart and Frank Morley. This young team built up a comprehensive and profitable catalogue distinguished by modern design, much of which is still in print. Biographies, memoirs, fiction, poetry, political and religious essays, art and architecture monographs, children's books and a pioneering range of ecology titles contributed towards an eclectic list full of character. Faber also produced Eliot's groundbreaking literary review *The Criterion*.

The Second World War brought both paper shortages and higher taxes, and the post-war years continued to be difficult. However, as the economy recovered a new generation of writers joined Faber, including William Golding, Robert Lowell, Ted Hughes, Sylvia Plath, Seamus Heaney, Philip Larkin, Thom Gunn and P. D. James. The publishing of Samuel Beckett and John Osborne began the firm's commitment to a modern drama list that now includes Tom Stoppard, Harold Pinter and David Hare.

From the 1970s through to the 1990s there was a blossoming in literary fiction, with the addition of authors such as Peter Carey, Kazuo Ishiguro, Barbara Kingsolver, Milan Kundera, Mario Vargas Llosa and Orhan Pamuk.

The year 2019 finds the publishing company that Geoffrey Faber founded remaining true to the principles he instigated and independent of corporate ownership. In its ninety years of publishing, Faber & Faber can count among its authors seven Carnegie Medal winners, three Kate Greenaway Medal winners, more than twenty Whitbread/Costa Book Award winners, six Man Booker Prize winners, twelve Forward Poetry Prize winners, and thirteen Nobel Laureates.

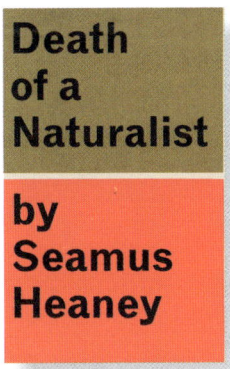

In addition to dedicated core publishing, recent years have seen some new strands emerge, including a distinctive Faber Audio list, the launch of the Faber Academy writing school and a Faber Members programme.

A more detailed chronology of Faber & Faber's poetry publishing appears at the back of this diary.

JANUARY

M	T	W	T	F	S	S
31	1	2	3	4	5	6
7	8	9	10	11	12	13
14	15	16	17	18	19	20
21	22	23	24	25	26	27
28	29	30	31	1	2	3
4	5	6	7	8	9	10

FEBRUARY

M	T	W	T	F	S	S
28	29	30	31	1	2	3
4	5	6	7	8	9	10
11	12	13	14	15	16	17
18	19	20	21	22	23	24
25	26	27	28	1	2	3
4	5	6	7	8	9	10

MARCH

M	T	W	T	F	S	S
25	26	27	28	1	2	3
4	5	6	7	8	9	10
11	12	13	14	15	16	17
18	19	20	21	22	23	24
25	26	27	28	29	30	31
1	2	3	4	5	6	7

APRIL

M	T	W	T	F	S	S
25	26	27	28	29	30	31
1	2	3	4	5	6	7
8	9	10	11	12	13	14
15	16	17	18	19	20	21
22	23	24	25	26	27	28
29	30	1	2	3	4	5

MAY

M	T	W	T	F	S	S
29	30	1	2	3	4	5
6	7	8	9	10	11	12
13	14	15	16	17	18	19
20	21	22	23	24	25	26
27	28	29	30	31	1	2
3	4	5	6	7	8	9

JUNE

M	T	W	T	F	S	S
27	28	29	30	31	1	2
3	4	5	6	7	8	9
10	11	12	13	14	15	16
17	18	19	20	21	22	23
24	25	26	27	28	29	30
1	2	3	4	5	6	7

JULY

M	T	W	T	F	S	S
24	25	26	27	28	29	30
1	2	3	4	5	6	7
8	9	10	11	12	13	14
15	16	17	18	19	20	21
22	23	24	25	26	27	28
29	30	31	1	2	3	4

AUGUST

M	T	W	T	F	S	S
29	30	31	1	2	3	4
5	6	7	8	9	10	11
12	13	14	15	16	17	18
19	20	21	22	23	24	25
26	27	28	29	30	31	1
2	3	4	5	6	7	8

SEPTEMBER

M	T	W	T	F	S	S
26	27	28	29	30	31	1
2	3	4	5	6	7	8
9	10	11	12	13	14	15
16	17	18	19	20	21	22
23	24	25	26	27	28	29
30	1	2	3	4	5	6

OCTOBER

M	T	W	T	F	S	S
30	1	2	3	4	5	6
7	8	9	10	11	12	13
14	15	16	17	18	19	20
21	22	23	24	25	26	27
28	29	30	31	1	2	3
4	5	6	7	8	9	10

NOVEMBER

M	T	W	T	F	S	S
28	29	30	31	1	2	3
4	5	6	7	8	9	10
11	12	13	14	15	16	17
18	19	20	21	22	23	24
25	26	27	28	29	30	1
2	3	4	5	6	7	8

DECEMBER

M	T	W	T	F	S	S
25	26	27	28	29	30	1
2	3	4	5	6	7	8
9	10	11	12	13	14	15
16	17	18	19	20	21	22
23	24	25	26	27	28	29
30	31	1	2	3	4	5

2018

JANUARY

M	T	W	T	F	S	S
1	2	3	4	5	6	7
8	9	10	11	12	13	14
15	16	17	18	19	20	21
22	23	24	25	26	27	28
29	30	31	1	2	3	4
5	6	7	8	9	10	11

FEBRUARY

M	T	W	T	F	S	S
29	30	31	1	2	3	4
5	6	7	8	9	10	11
12	13	14	15	16	17	18
19	20	21	22	23	24	25
26	27	28	1	2	3	4
5	6	7	8	9	10	11

MARCH

M	T	W	T	F	S	S
26	27	28	1	2	3	4
5	6	7	8	9	10	11
12	13	14	15	16	17	18
19	20	21	22	23	24	25
26	27	28	29	30	31	1
2	3	4	5	6	7	8

APRIL

M	T	W	T	F	S	S
26	27	28	29	30	31	1
2	3	4	5	6	7	8
9	10	11	12	13	14	15
16	17	18	19	20	21	22
23	24	25	26	27	28	29
30	1	2	3	4	5	6

MAY

M	T	W	T	F	S	S
30	1	2	3	4	5	6
7	8	9	10	11	12	13
14	15	16	17	18	19	20
21	22	23	24	25	26	27
28	29	30	31	1	2	3
4	5	6	7	8	9	10

JUNE

M	T	W	T	F	S	S
28	29	30	31	1	2	3
4	5	6	7	8	9	10
11	12	13	14	15	16	17
18	19	20	21	22	23	24
25	26	27	28	29	30	1
2	3	4	5	6	7	8

JULY

M	T	W	T	F	S	S
25	26	27	28	29	30	1
2	3	4	5	6	7	8
9	10	11	12	13	14	15
16	17	18	19	20	21	22
23	24	25	26	27	28	29
30	31	1	2	3	4	5

AUGUST

M	T	W	T	F	S	S
30	31	1	2	3	4	5
6	7	8	9	10	11	12
13	14	15	16	17	18	19
20	21	22	23	24	25	26
27	28	29	30	31	1	2
3	4	5	6	7	8	9

SEPTEMBER

M	T	W	T	F	S	S
27	28	29	30	31	1	2
3	4	5	6	7	8	9
10	11	12	13	14	15	16
17	18	19	20	21	22	23
24	25	26	27	28	29	30
1	2	3	4	5	6	7

OCTOBER

M	T	W	T	F	S	S
1	2	3	4	5	6	7
8	9	10	11	12	13	14
15	16	17	18	19	20	21
22	23	24	25	26	27	28
29	30	31	1	2	3	4
5	6	7	8	9	10	11

NOVEMBER

M	T	W	T	F	S	S
29	30	31	1	2	3	4
5	6	7	8	9	10	11
12	13	14	15	16	17	18
19	20	21	22	23	24	25
26	27	28	29	30	1	2
3	4	5	6	7	8	9

DECEMBER

M	T	W	T	F	S	S
26	27	28	29	30	1	2
3	4	5	6	7	8	9
10	11	12	13	14	15	16
17	18	19	20	21	22	23
24	25	26	27	28	29	30
31	1	2	3	4	5	6

2020

JANUARY

M	T	W	T	F	S	S
30	31	1	2	3	4	5
6	7	8	9	10	11	12
13	14	15	16	17	18	19
20	21	22	23	24	25	26
27	28	29	30	31	1	2
3	4	5	6	7	8	9

FEBRUARY

M	T	W	T	F	S	S
27	28	29	30	31	1	2
3	4	5	6	7	8	9
10	11	12	13	14	15	16
17	18	19	20	21	22	23
24	25	26	27	28	29	1
2	3	4	5	6	7	8

MARCH

M	T	W	T	F	S	S
24	25	26	27	28	29	1
2	3	4	5	6	7	8
9	10	11	12	13	14	15
16	17	18	19	20	21	22
23	24	25	26	27	28	29
30	31	1	2	3	4	5

APRIL

M	T	W	T	F	S	S
30	31	1	2	3	4	5
6	7	8	9	10	11	12
13	14	15	16	17	18	19
20	21	22	23	24	25	26
27	28	29	30	1	2	3
4	5	6	7	8	9	10

MAY

M	T	W	T	F	S	S
27	28	29	30	1	2	3
4	5	6	7	8	9	10
11	12	13	14	15	16	17
18	19	20	21	22	23	24
25	26	27	28	29	30	31
1	2	3	4	5	6	7

JUNE

M	T	W	T	F	S	S
1	2	3	4	5	6	7
8	9	10	11	12	13	14
15	16	17	18	19	20	21
22	23	24	25	26	27	28
29	30	1	2	3	4	5
6	7	8	9	10	11	12

JULY

M	T	W	T	F	S	S
29	30	1	2	3	4	5
6	7	8	9	10	11	12
13	14	15	16	17	18	19
20	21	22	23	24	25	26
27	28	29	30	31	1	2
3	4	5	6	7	8	9

AUGUST

M	T	W	T	F	S	S
27	28	29	30	31	1	2
3	4	5	6	7	8	9
10	11	12	13	14	15	16
17	18	19	20	21	22	23
24	25	26	27	28	29	30
31	1	2	3	4	5	6

SEPTEMBER

M	T	W	T	F	S	S
31	1	2	3	4	5	6
7	8	9	10	11	12	13
14	15	16	17	18	19	20
21	22	23	24	25	26	27
28	29	30	1	2	3	4
5	6	7	8	9	10	11

OCTOBER

M	T	W	T	F	S	S
28	29	30	1	2	3	4
5	6	7	8	9	10	11
12	13	14	15	16	17	18
19	20	21	22	23	24	25
26	27	28	29	30	31	1
2	3	4	5	6	7	8

NOVEMBER

M	T	W	T	F	S	S
26	27	28	29	30	31	1
2	3	4	5	6	7	8
9	10	11	12	13	14	15
16	17	18	19	20	21	22
23	24	25	26	27	28	29
30	1	2	3	4	5	6

DECEMBER

M	T	W	T	F	S	S
30	1	2	3	4	5	6
7	8	9	10	11	12	13
14	15	16	17	18	19	20
21	22	23	24	25	26	27
28	29	30	31	1	2	3
4	5	6	7	8	9	10

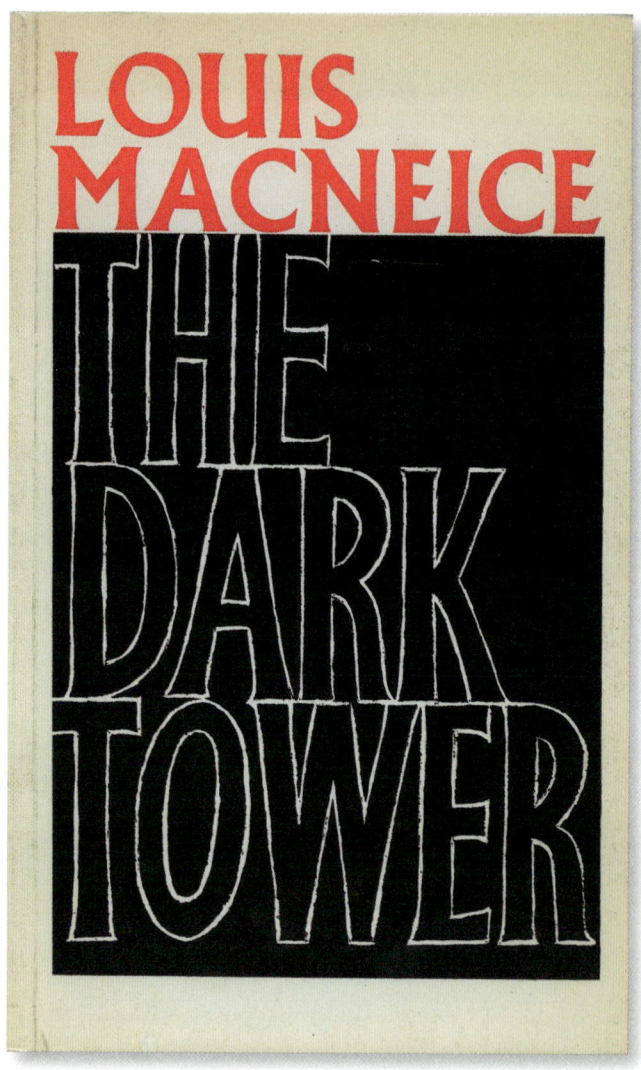

31 Monday

1 Tuesday NEW YEAR'S DAY HOLIDAY (UK, IRL, AUS, ZA, NZ, CAN, USA)

2 Wednesday 2ND JANUARY HOLIDAY (SCT)
DAY AFTER NEW YEAR'S DAY (NZ)

3 Thursday

4 Friday

5 Saturday

6 Sunday

Inversnaid

This darksome burn, horseback brown,
His rollrock highroad roaring down,
In coop and in comb the fleece of his foam
Flutes and low to the lake falls home.

A windpuff-bonnet of fáwn-fróth
Turns and twindles over the broth
Of a pool so pitchblack, féll-frówning,
It rounds and rounds Despair to drowning.

Degged with dew, dappled with dew
Are the groins of the braes that the brook treads through,
Wiry heathpacks, flitches of fern,
And the beadbonny ash that sits over the burn.

What would the world be, once bereft
Of wet and of wildness? Let them be left,
O let them be left, wildness and wet;
Long live the weeds and the wilderness yet.

POET TO POET *Gerard Manley Hopkins: Poems Selected by John Stammers* (2012)

7 Monday

8 Tuesday

9 Wednesday

10 Thursday

11 Friday

12 Saturday   13 Sunday

The Crotchet

The trick you had on occasion,
mid-embrace,
of using the tip of my nose
to push your slipped spectacles
back up the slope of your nose
to their proper place:
I could never on the spot
decide whether I should be
amused or irritated;
and — you know what? —
only now do I see
how neither response was right,
and that I was simply an uptight,
slow-on-the-uptake
beneficiary of your grace.

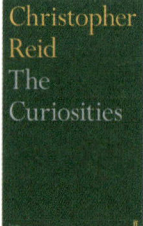

The Curiosities (2015)

14 Monday

15 Tuesday

16 Wednesday

17 Thursday

18 Friday

19 Saturday   20 Sunday

Song

Ae fond kiss, and then we sever;
Ae farewell, and then for ever!
Deep in heart-wrung tears I'll pledge thee,
Warring sighs and groans I'll wage thee. –

Who shall say that Fortune grieves him,
While the star of hope she leaves him:
Me, nae cheerful twinkle lights me;
Dark despair around benights me. –

I'll ne'er blame my partial fancy,
Naething could resist my Nancy:
But to see her, was to love her;
Love but her, and love for ever. –

Had we never lov'd sae kindly,
Had we never lov'd sae blindly!
Never met – or never parted,
We had ne'er been broken-hearted. –

Fare-thee-weel, thou first and fairest!
Fare-thee-weel, thou best and dearest!
Thine be ilka joy and treasure,
Peace, Enjoyment, Love and Pleasure! –

Ae fond kiss, and then we sever!
Ae fareweel, Alas, for ever!
Deep in heart-wrung tears I'll pledge thee,
Warring sighs and groans I'll wage thee. –

POET TO POET *Robert Burns: Poems Selected by Don Paterson* (2005)

21 Monday   MARTIN LUTHER KING DAY (USA)

22 Tuesday

23 Wednesday

24 Thursday

25 Friday   BURNS NIGHT

26 Saturday   AUSTRALIA DAY   27 Sunday

Hannah Sullivan

Three Poems

ff

28 Monday AUSTRALIA DAY HOLIDAY (AUS)

29 Tuesday

30 Wednesday

31 Thursday

1 Friday

2 Saturday   3 Sunday

Sonnet 12

When I do count the clock that tells the time,
And see the brave day sunk in hideous night;
When I behold the violet past prime,
And sable curls all silvered o'er with white;
When lofty trees I see barren of leaves,
Which erst from heat did canopy the herd,
And summer's green all girded up in sheaves
Borne on the bier with white and bristly beard:
Then of thy beauty do I question make,
That thou among the wastes of time must go,
Since sweets and beauties do themselves forsake
And die as fast as they see others grow,
　　And nothing 'gainst Time's scythe can make defence
　　Save breed to brave him when he takes thee hence.

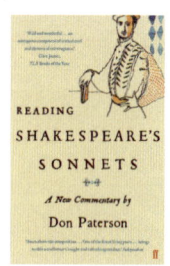

Reading Shakespeare's Sonnets: A New Commentary (2010)

4 Monday

5 Tuesday

6 Wednesday   WAITANGI DAY (NZ)

7 Thursday

8 Friday

9 Saturday   10 Sunday

Roe-deer

In the dawn-dirty light, in the biggest snow of the year
Two blue-dark deer stood in the road, alerted.

They had happened into my dimension
The moment I was arriving just there.

They planted their two or three years of secret deerhood
Clear on my snow-screen vision of the abnormal

And hesitated in the all-way disintegration
And stared at me. And so for some lasting seconds

I could think the deer were waiting for me
To remember the password and sign

That the curtain had blown aside for a moment
And there where the trees were no longer trees, nor the road a road

The deer had come for me.

Then they ducked through the hedge, and upright they rode their legs
Away downhill over a snow-lonely field

Towards tree dark – finally
Seeming to eddy and glide and fly away up

Into the boil of big flakes.
The snow took them and soon their nearby hoofprints as well

Revising its dawn inspiration
Back to the ordinary.

Ted
Hughes
Moortown
Diary

Moortown Diary (1979)

11 Monday

---

12 Tuesday LINCOLN'S BIRTHDAY

---

13 Wednesday

---

14 Thursday VALENTINE'S DAY

---

15 Friday

---

16 Saturday   17 Sunday

The Slim Man

A landscape unpainted:
a cold stream of lean black weeds
leading towards a stile
and a field tilting up.
Trees turn to veins against marbly sky
in the half hour before night.

During a certain moon
children are said to have seen
a slim man walking over the field
in a low mist, towards the stile,
leading a girl
in pale blue pinstripes
into the glowing pinstripe forest beyond.

Sometimes he will stop and lean down,
and scrape the earth,
then earth and touch are knotted
for they are both cold.
No one is scared of him,
more of the thick dark brook, drowned roots
and full night, the pitiful rabbits'
eyes yellow on the hillside.

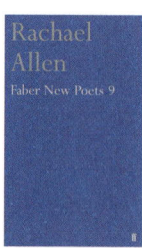

Faber New Poets 9 (2014)

18 **Monday** PRESIDENTS' DAY (USA)

---

19 Tuesday

---

20 Wednesday

---

21 Thursday

---

22 Friday

---

23 Saturday   24 Sunday

Dorothy
Molloy

Hare Soup

Poetry

25 Monday

26 Tuesday

27 Wednesday

28 Thursday

1 Friday ST DAVID'S DAY

2 Saturday   3 Sunday

The Net-Menders

Halfway up from the little harbor of sardine boats,
Halfway down from groves where the thin, bitter almond pips
Fatten in green-pocked pods, the three net-menders sit out,
Dressed in black, everybody in mourning for someone.
They set their stout chairs back to the road and face the dark
Dominoes of their doorways.

                      Sun grains their crow-colors,
Purples the fig in the leaf's shadow, turns the dust pink.
On the road named for Tomas Ortunio, mica
Winks like money under the ringed toes of the chickens.
The houses are white as sea-salt goats lick from the rocks.

While their fingers work with the coarse mesh and the fine
Their eyes revolve the whole town like a blue and green ball.
Nobody dies or is born without their knowing it.
They talk of bride-lace, of lovers spunky as gamecocks.

The moon leans, a stone madonna, over the lead sea
And the iron hills that enclose them. Earthen fingers
Twist old words into the web-threads:

                        Tonight may the fish
Be a harvest of silver in the nets, and the lamps
Of our husbands and sons move sure among the low stars.

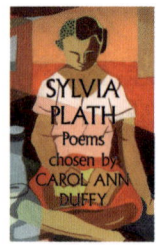

Sylvia Plath: Poems Chosen by Carol Ann Duffy (2012)

4 Monday

5 Tuesday

6 Wednesday

7 Thursday

8 Friday

9 Saturday   10 Sunday

The Unaccompanied

Wandering slowly back after dark one night
above a river, towards a suspension bridge,
a sound concerns him that might be a tune
or might not: noise drifting in, trailing off.

Then concerns him again, now clearly a song
pulsing out from the opposite bank, being sung
by chorusing men, all pewter-haired or bald,
in the function suite of a shabby hotel.
Above their heads a conductor's hand
draws and casts the notes with a white wand.

Songs about mills and mines and a great war,
about mermaid brides and solid gold hills,
songs from broken hymnbooks and cheesy films.

Then his father's voice rising out of that choir,
and his father's father's voice, and voices
of fathers before, concerning him only,
arcing through charged air and spanning the gorge.
He steps over the cliff edge and walks across.

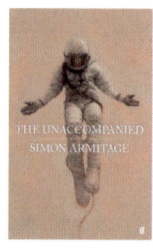

The Unaccompanied (2017)

11 Monday

12 Tuesday

13 Wednesday

14 Thursday

15 Friday

16 Saturday

17 Sunday ST PATRICK'S DAY

Never love unlesse you can

Never love unlesse you can
Beare with all the faults of man:
Men sometimes will jealous bee
Though but little cause they see,
 And hang the head, as discontent,
 And speake what straight they will repent.

Men that but one Saint adore
Make a shew of love to more:
Beauty must be scorn'd in none,
Though but truely serv'd in one:
 For what is courtship, but disguise?
 True hearts may have dissembling eyes.

Men, when their affaires require,
Must a while themselves retire:
Sometimes hunt, and sometimes hawke,
And not ever sit and talke.
 If these, and such like, you can beare,
 Then like, and love, and never feare.

POET TO POET *Thomas Campion: Poems Selected by Charles Simic* (2007)

18 Monday ST PATRICK'S DAY HOLIDAY (IRL, NI)

19 Tuesday

20 Wednesday

21 Thursday HUMAN RIGHTS DAY (ZA)

22 Friday

23 Saturday 24 Sunday

LIKE A
BULWARK

NEW
POEMS BY
MARIANNE
MOORE
FABER AND
FABER

LIKE A
BULWARK

25 Monday

26 Tuesday

27 Wednesday

28 Thursday

29 Friday

30 Saturday   31 Sunday

My heart leaps up when I behold

My heart leaps up when I behold
   A rainbow in the sky:
So was it when my life began;
So is it now I am a man;
So be it when I shall grow old,
   Or let me die!
The Child is father of the Man;
And I could wish my days to be
Bound each to each by natural piety.

POET TO POET *William Wordsworth: Poems Selected by Seamus Heaney* (2001)

1 Monday

2 Tuesday

3 Wednesday

4 Thursday

5 Friday

6 Saturday

7 Sunday

To a Bed of Tulips

Bright Tulips, we do know,
You had your comming hither;
And Fading-time do's show,
That Ye must quickly wither.

Your Sister-hoods may stay,
And smile here or your houre;
But dye ye must away:
Even as the meanest Flower.

Come Virgins then, and see
Your frailties; and bemone ye;
For lost like these, 'twill be,
As Time had never known ye.

POET TO POET *Robert Herrick: Poems Selected by Stephen Romer* (2010)

8 Monday

9 Tuesday

10 Wednesday

11 Thursday

12 Friday

13 Saturday

14 Sunday

In the Fields

Lord, when I look at lovely things which pass,
    Under old trees the shadows of young leaves
Dancing to please the wind along the grass,
    Or the gold stillness of the August sun on the
        August sheaves;
Can I believe there is a heavenlier world than this?
    And if there is
Will the strange heart of any everlasting thing
    Bring me these dreams that take my breath away?
They come at evening with the home-flying rooks
    and the scent of hay,
        Over the fields. They come in spring.

POETRY PLEASE: *The Seasons* (2015)

15 Monday   TAX DAY (USA)

16 Tuesday

17 Wednesday

18 Thursday

19 Friday   GOOD FRIDAY (UK, AUS, ZA, NZ, CAN)

20 Saturday   EASTER (HOLY) SATURDAY   21 Sunday   EASTER SUNDAY

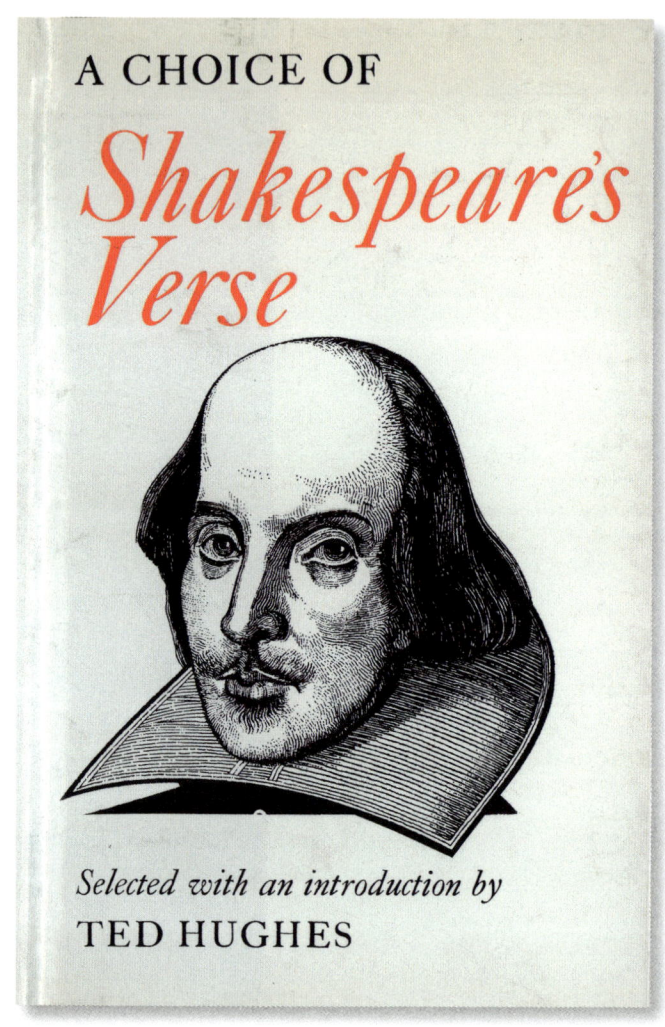

A CHOICE OF

Shakespeare's Verse

Selected with an introduction by
TED HUGHES

22 Monday   EASTER MONDAY (UK NOT SCT, IRL, AUS, NZ)

FAMILY DAY (ZA)

23 Tuesday   ST GEORGE'S DAY

24 Wednesday

25 Thursday   ANZAC DAY (AUS, NZ)

26 Friday

27 Saturday   FREEDOM DAY (ZA)   28 Sunday

A double sorrow

A sad story is sad to tell
But if it makes some part of sadness clear
To those who've suffered then it's real and therefore
True and we who've suffered can trace the shape
Of our own despair and so the shadow lifts
Leaving an outline that could be anyone's.
Take it or make it mine.

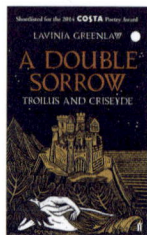

A Double Sorrow (2014)

29 Monday

30 Tuesday

1 Wednesday   WORKERS' DAY (ZA)

2 Thursday

3 Friday

4 Saturday   5 Sunday

Prelude to the Afternoon of a Faun

Noon ictus cooling the veranda's
fretwork, the child sits after his harp
boning burlesque in the bower, his slit
of gulls' nerves silenced into hydrangea.
Violet and roan, the bridal sun is
opening and closing a window,
filling a clay pot of coins with coins;
candle jars, a crystal globe, cut milk
boxes with horn petals snapping
their iceberg-Golgotha crackle.
The loneliness is terrible, the ice is near,
says the hasp-lipped devil, casting
beatitudes at the castor-oiled pimps
in Parliament; Pray for them, joyfully,
their amazing death! Light seethes
bulging like pipes blown with napalm
from his big golden eyes, turning
the afternoon ten degrees backwards,
then through palm fronds' teething
the bridled air, sprigs of goat hair, fall.

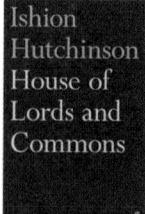

House of Lords and Commons (2017)

6 Monday   EARLY MAY BANK HOLIDAY (UK), MAY DAY (IRL)

7 Tuesday

8 Wednesday

9 Thursday

10 Friday

11 Saturday   12 Sunday

Written after Swimming from Sestos to Abydos

If, in the month of dark December,
    Leander, who was nightly wont
(What maid will not the tale remember?)
    To cross thy stream, broad Hellespont!

If, when the wintry tempest roar'd,
    He sped to Hero, nothing loth,
And thus of old thy current pour'd,
    Fair Venus! How I pity both!

For *me*, degenerate modern wretch,
    Though in the genial month of May,
My dripping limbs I fairly stretch,
    And think I've done a feat to-day.

But since he cross'd the rapid tide,
    According to the doubtful story,
To woo, – and – Lord knows what beside,
    And swam for Love, as I for Glory;

'Twere hard to say who fared the best:
    Sad mortals! thus the gods still plague you!
He lost his labour, I my jest;
    For he was drown'd, and I've the ague.

POET TO POET *Lord Byron: Poems Selected by Paul Muldoon* (2007)

13 Monday

14 Tuesday

15 Wednesday

16 Thursday

17 Friday

18 Saturday   19 Sunday

ST. KILDA'S PARLIAMENT

Douglas Dunn

20 Monday

21 Tuesday

22 Wednesday

23 Thursday

24 Friday

25 Saturday   26 Sunday

The Apparition

When by thy scorne, O murdresse, I am dead,
And that thou thinkst thee free
From all solicitation from mee,
Then shall my ghost come to thy bed,
And thee, fain'd vestall, in worse armes shall see;
Then thy sicke taper will begin to winke,
And he, whose thou art then, being tyr'd before,
Will, if thou stirre, or pinch to wake him, thinke
      Thou call'st for more,
And in false sleepe will from thee shrinke,
And then poore Aspen wretch, neglected thou
Bath'd in a cold quicksilver sweat wilt lye
      A veryer ghost then I;
What I will say, I will not tell thee now,
Lest that preserve thee; and since my love is spent,
I had rather thou shouldst painfully repent,
Then by my threatnings rest still innocent.

27 Monday   SPRING BANK HOLIDAY (UK), MEMORIAL DAY (USA)

28 Tuesday

29 Wednesday

30 Thursday

31 Friday

1 Saturday   2 Sunday

'Now welcome, somer, with thy sonne softe'

from The Parliament of Fowls

Now welcome, somer, with thy sonne softe,
That hast this wintres wedres overshake,
And driven away the longe nyghtes blake!

Saynt Valentyn, that art ful hy on-lofte,
Thus syngen smale foules for thy sake:
Now welcome, somer, with thy sonne softe,
That hast this wintres wedres overshake.

Wel han they cause for to gladen ofte,
Sith ech of hem recovered hath hys make;
Ful blissful mowe they synge when they wake:
Now welcome, somer, with thy sonne softe
That hast this wintres wedres overshake
And driven away the longe nyghtes blake!

POETRY PLEASE: *The Seasons* (2015)

3 Monday JUNE BANK HOLIDAY (IRL), QUEEN'S BIRTHDAY HOLIDAY (NZ)

4 Tuesday

5 Wednesday

6 Thursday

7 Friday

8 Saturday   9 Sunday

Self-Portrait on The Levels

A field of water the sun stares up
from with cold, undiminished ferocity.
Unconscious of its own image
in the wind breaking, breaking and re-
forming, how barely it seems to live
the automatic and suicidal gift
of its self-burning, the blind necessity
of love, broken and re-forming.
The elegant feathers of grass bow to it
coyly, above a flight of ducks in-
carnadine as nipple-heads, their under-
sides beating to the rush of shot.
Uncoppiced, a line of Black Mauls
wanders to the horizon, trailing fingers
through the surface of a rare heaven —
as if patiently for the season when
they shall be hurdles, and withy men.

Toby
Martinez
de las Rivas
Faber New Poets 2

Faber New Poets 2 (2009)

10 Monday

11 Tuesday

12 Wednesday

13 Thursday

14 Friday

15 Saturday   16 Sunday   YOUTH DAY (ZA)

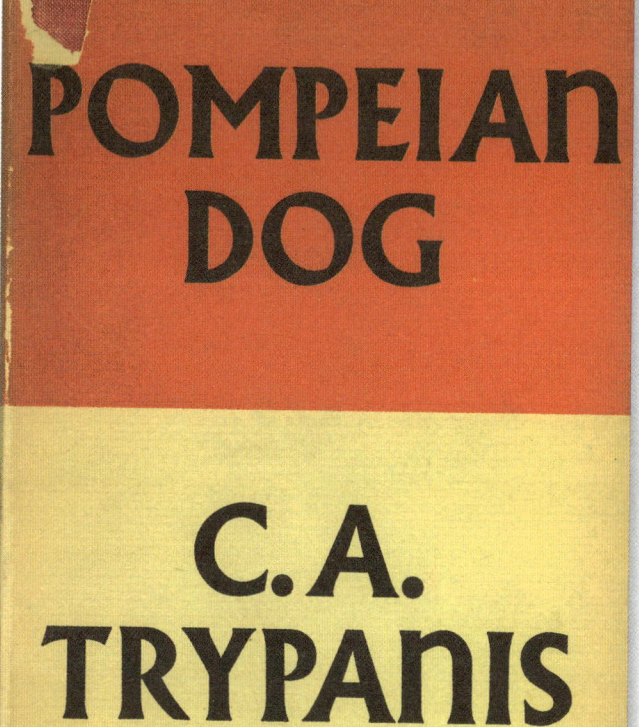

17 Monday   YOUTH DAY HOLIDAY (ZA)

18 Tuesday

19 Wednesday

20 Thursday

21 Friday

22 Saturday   23 Sunday

Cut Grass

Cut grass lies frail:
Brief is the breath
Mown stalks exhale.
Long, long the death

It dies in the white hours
Of young-leafed June
With chestnut flowers,
With hedges snowlike strewn,

White lilac bowed,
Lost lanes of Queen Anne's lace,
And that high-builded cloud
Moving at summer's pace.

Philip Larkin: The Complete Poems (2012)

24 Monday

---

25 Tuesday

---

26 Wednesday

---

27 Thursday

---

28 Friday

---

29 Saturday   30 Sunday

le jardin secret

boys were my saplings
my whiff of green my sprouts
a hundred soft palms
reaching for my warmth
boys were my herbs
square-stemmed furred
scented with musk dank clove
& lovage boys were my
crops my ripe-red-yield
my seeds each one exploding
onto my lips like sherbet
boys were my vines my
creepers my climbers
tattooing my neck back
& thighs with suckle boys
were my nettles my thistles
my thorns tickling me with
scratches & painting me
scarlet boys were my berries
my doll's eyes my yew
bitter on the tongue dizzying
& psychedelic boys were my
pitchers my fly-traps my
venus a petalled mouth wet
throat around a grave

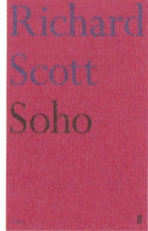

Soho (2018)

1 Monday CANADA DAY (CAN)

2 Tuesday

3 Wednesday

4 Thursday INDEPENDENCE DAY (USA)

5 Friday

6 Saturday   7 Sunday

Beans in Blossom

The south-west wind, how pleasant in the face
It breathes, while sauntering in a musing pace
I roam these new-ploughed fields, and by the side
Of this old wood where happy birds abide
And the rich blackbird through his golden bill
Utters wild music when the rest are still:
Now luscious comes the scent of blossomed beans
That o'er the path in rich disorder leans,
Mid which the bees in busy songs and toils
Load home luxuriantly their yellow spoils;
The herd cows toss the molehills in their play;
And often stand the stranger's steps at bay
Mid clover blossoms red and tawny-white,
Strong-scented with the summer's warm delight.

POET TO POET *John Clare: Poems Selected by Paul Farley* (2007)

8 Monday

9 Tuesday

10 Wednesday

11 Thursday

12 Friday BATTLE OF THE BOYNE HOLIDAY (NI)

13 Saturday   14 Sunday

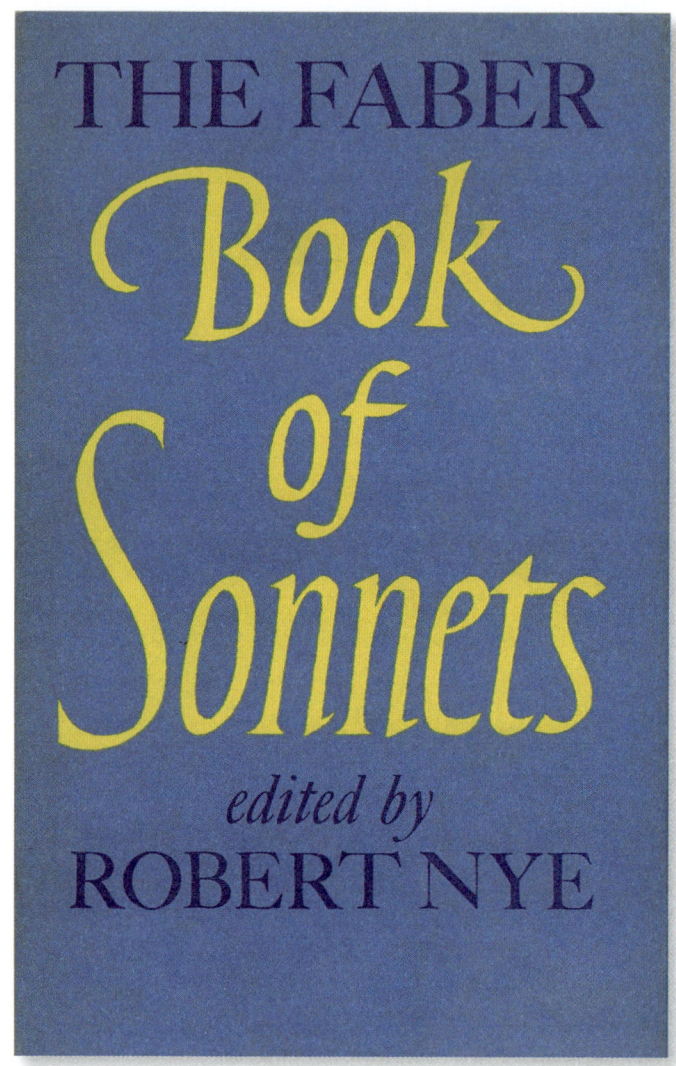

THE FABER
Book
of
Sonnets

edited by
ROBERT NYE

15 Monday

---

16 Tuesday

---

17 Wednesday

---

18 Thursday

---

19 Friday

---

20 Saturday   21 Sunday

Correctives

The shudder in my son's left hand
he cures with one touch from his right,
two fingertips laid feather-light
to still his pen. He understands

the whole man must be his own brother
for no man is himself alone;
though some of us have never known
the one hand's kindness to the other.

Don Paterson: Selected Poems (2012)

22 Monday

---

23 Tuesday

---

24 Wednesday

---

25 Thursday

---

26 Friday

---

27 Saturday   28 Sunday

For Summer

The lie is light over your heart.
You will do nothing about it.
The swallows are chattering
around the house. All night
you sweat it out waiting for a breeze
to collapse you to sleep.

You lay down in front of your door,
your head pointing north, but
none of the other cardinal points
creep into your body. Your ears,
loosened with olive oil, tune into
difficult stars, loud and hot.

Summer is going. You are already
running into the first snowflake,
mouth open to taste it, primed
to ingest all the weathers.

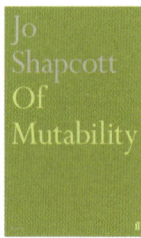

Of Mutability (2010)

29 Monday

30 Tuesday

31 Wednesday

1 Thursday

2 Friday

3 Saturday   4 Sunday

Lightenings

viii

The annals say: when the monks of Clonmacnoise
Were all at prayers inside the oratory
A ship appeared above them in the air.

The anchor dragged along behind so deep
It hooked itself into the altar rails
And then, as the big hull rocked to a standstill,

A crewman shinned and grappled down the rope
And struggled to release it. But in vain.
'This man can't bear our life here and will drown,'

The abbot said, 'unless we help him.' So
They did, the freed ship sailed, and the man climbed back
Out of the marvellous as he had known it.

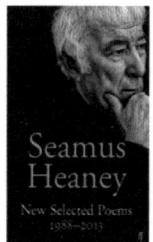

Seamus Heaney: New Selected Poems 1988–2013 (2014)

5 Monday   AUGUST BANK HOLIDAY (IRL.)

6 Tuesday

7 Wednesday

8 Thursday

9 Friday   NATIONAL WOMEN'S DAY (ZA)

10 Saturday   11 Sunday

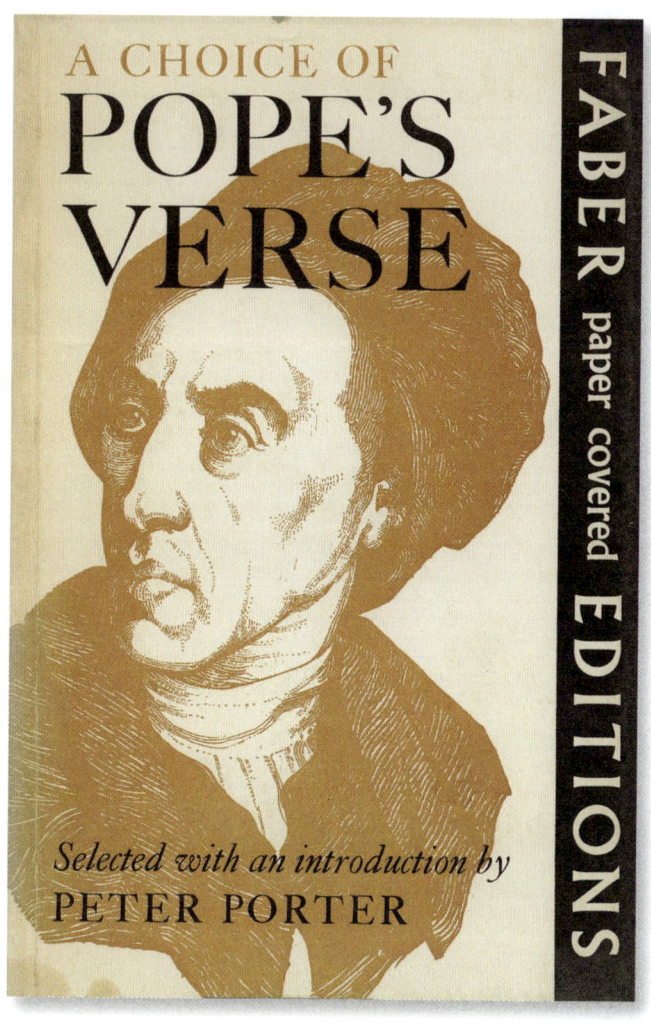

A CHOICE OF
POPE'S
VERSE

Selected with an introduction by
PETER PORTER

FABER paper covered EDITIONS

12 Monday

13 Tuesday

14 Wednesday

15 Thursday

16 Friday

17 Saturday 18 Sunday

54

This page is a cloud between whose fraying edges
a headland with mountains appears brokenly
then is hidden again until what emerges
from the now cloudless blue is the grooved sea
and the whole self-naming island, its ochre verges,
its shadow-plunged valleys and a coiled road
threading the fishing villages, the white, silent surges
of combers along the coast, where a line of gulls has arrowed
into the widening harbor of a town with no noise,
its streets growing closer like print you can now read,
two cruise ships, schooners, a tug, ancestral canoes,
as a cloud slowly covers the page and it goes
white again and the book comes to a close.

The Poetry of Derek Walcott 1948–2013 (2014)

19 Monday

20 Tuesday

21 Wednesday

22 Thursday

23 Friday

24 Saturday   25 Sunday

Father of Only Daughters

Thousand times or more tonight
now you're in a big-girl bed
and it's mum's rare night out
I've simply flown upstairs

to watch you upside down again.
I'm so *oh* over my head
knowing you're safe at this stage
behind your bed-guard.

Two years old, already a clown,
you're the jumping sidekick
to your bigger sister
who's kicked off her duvet again.

In my past, I was treated
as a child when I was a man
and forced to remain in wedlock
to uphold the family name.

Look at me flying upstairs
on the wings of my shame
for my second-chance life.
A life under yours in a fall.

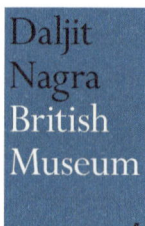

Daljit
Nagra
British
Museum

British Museum (2017)

26 Monday SUMMER BANK HOLIDAY (UK)

27 Tuesday

28 Wednesday

29 Thursday

30 Friday

31 Saturday   1 Sunday

A Birthday

My heart is like a singing bird
　　Whose nest is in a watered shoot;
My heart is like an apple tree
　　Whose boughs are bent with thickset fruit;
My heart is like a rainbow shell
　　That paddles in a halcyon sea;
My heart is gladder than all these
　　Because my love is come to me.

Raise me a dais of silk and down;
　　Hang it with vair and purple dyes;
Carve it in doves and pomegranates,
　　And peacocks with a hundred eyes;
Work it in gold and silver grapes,
　　In leaves and silver fleurs-de-lys;
Because the birthday of my life
　　Is come, my love is come to me.

2 Monday   LABOR DAY (USA), LABOUR DAY (CAN)

---

3 Tuesday

---

4 Wednesday

---

5 Thursday

---

6 Friday

---

7 Saturday   8 Sunday

HIGH ISLAND

RICHARD MURPHY

9 Monday

10 Tuesday

11 Wednesday

12 Thursday

13 Friday

14 Saturday   15 Sunday

'Fall, leaves, fall'

Fall, leaves, fall; die, flowers, away;
Lengthen night and shorten day;
Every leaf speaks bliss to me,
Fluttering from the autumn tree.

I shall smile when wreaths of snow
Blossom where the rose should grow;
I shall sing when night's decay
Ushers in a drearier day.

16 Monday

17 Tuesday

18 Wednesday

19 Thursday

20 Friday

21 Saturday   22 Sunday

An Irish Airman Foresees His Death

I know that I shall meet my fate
Somewhere among the clouds above;
Those that I fight I do not hate,
Those that I guard I do not love;
My country is Kiltartan Cross,
My countrymen Kiltartan's poor,
No likely end could bring them loss
Or leave them happier than before.
Nor law, nor duty bade me fight,
Nor public men, nor cheering crowds,
A lonely impulse of delight
Drove to this tumult in the clouds;
I balanced all, brought all to mind,
The years to come seemed waste of breath,
A waste of breath the years behind
In balance with this life, this death.

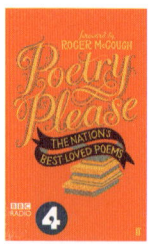

23 Monday

---

24 Tuesday   HERITAGE DAY (ZA)

---

25 Wednesday

---

26 Thursday

---

27 Friday

---

28 Saturday   29 Sunday

Weathers

This is the weather the cuckoo likes,
    And so do I;
When showers betumble the chestnut spikes,
    And nestlings fly:
And the little brown nightingale bills his best,
And they sit outside at 'The Travellers' Rest,'
And maids come forth sprig-muslin drest,
And citizens dream of the south and west,
    And so do I.

This is the weather the shepherd shuns,
    And so do I;
When beeches drip in browns and duns,
    And thresh, and ply;
And hill-hid tides throb, throe on throe,
And meadow rivulets overflow,
And drops on gate-bars hang in a row,
And rooks in families homeward go,
    And so do I.

POETRY PLEASE: *The Seasons* (2015)

30 Monday ROSH HASHANAH

1 Tuesday

2 Wednesday

3 Thursday

4 Friday

5 Saturday   6 Sunday

Seamus Heaney Beowulf

Poetry

ff

7 Monday

---

8 Tuesday

---

9 Wednesday   YOM KIPPUR

---

10 Thursday

---

11 Friday

---

12 Saturday   13 Sunday

IV. Death by Water

from The Waste Land

Phlebas the Phoenician, a fortnight dead,
Forgot the cry of gulls, and the deep sea swell
And the profit and loss.
                A current under sea
Picked his bones in whispers. As he rose and fell
He passed the stages of his age and youth
Entering the whirlpool.
                Gentile or Jew
O you who turn the wheel and look to windward,
Consider Phlebas, who was once handsome and tall as you.

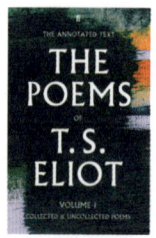

The Poems of T. S. Eliot Volume I (2015)

14 Monday THANKSGIVING DAY (CAN), COLUMBUS DAY (USA)

15 Tuesday

16 Wednesday

17 Thursday

18 Friday

19 Saturday   20 Sunday

I Had a Dove

I had a dove and the sweet dove died;
   And I have thought it died of grieving:
O, what could it grieve for? Its feet were tied,
   With a silken thread of my own hand's weaving;
   Sweet little red feet! why should you die –
Why should you leave me, sweet bird! Why?
You lived alone in the forest-tree,
Why, pretty thing! would you not live with me?
I kissed you oft and gave you white peas;
Why not live sweetly, as in the green trees?

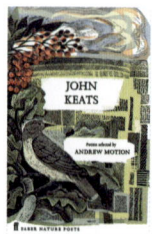

POET TO POET *John Keats: Poems Selected by Andrew Motion* (2000)

21 Monday

22 Tuesday

23 Wednesday

24 Thursday

25 Friday

26 Saturday   27 Sunday

Worship

When picking your spot, look for a balance
of elements. Always show respect to those
wearing lower factors than you. Always check
downwind before shaking out your towel.

Lie back. Let the sand make a duplicate
of your spine. Match your breath to the tide.
Clear away all thoughts (now that wasn't
so tough). Let your body do the thinking.

On the backs of your eyelids, you will likely
see your childhood sweetheart in flames,
dowsed in lamp oil. This is natural.
Let her dance. You deepen by the hour.

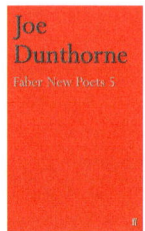

Faber New Poets 5 (2010)

28 Monday   OCTOBER BANK HOLIDAY (IRL)   LABOUR DAY (NZ)

29 Tuesday

30 Wednesday

31 Thursday   HALLOWEEN

1 Friday

2 Saturday   3 Sunday

'A guardian spirit of the
land and language.'
Seamus Heaney

TED
HUGHES
COLLECTED POEMS

4 Monday

5 Tuesday

6 Wednesday

7 Thursday

8 Friday

9 Saturday   10 Sunday   REMEMBRANCE SUNDAY

Ballad of the Three Spectres

As I went up by Ovillers
　　In mud and water cold to the knee,
There went three jeering, fleering spectres,
　　That walked abreast and talked of me.

The first said, 'Here's a right brave soldier
　　That walks the dark unfearingly;
Soon he'll come back on a fine stretcher,
　　And laughing for a nice Blighty.'

The second, 'Read his face, old comrade,
　　No kind of lucky chance I see;
One day he'll freeze in mud to the marrow,
　　Then look his last on Picardie.'

Though bitter the word of these first twain
　　Curses the third spat venomously;
'He'll stay untouched till the war's last dawning
　　Then live one hour of agony.'

Liars the first two were. Behold me
　　At sloping arms by one – two – three;
Waiting the time I shall discover
　　Whether the third spake verity.

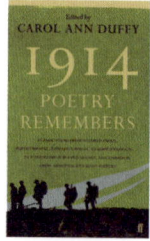

1914: Poetry Remembers edited by Carol Ann Duffy (2013)

11 Monday REMEMBRANCE DAY (CAN) VETERANS DAY (USA)

12 Tuesday

13 Wednesday

14 Thursday

15 Friday

16 Saturday   17 Sunday

Snow

In the gloom of whiteness,
In the great silence of snow,
A child was sighing
And bitterly saying: 'Oh,
They have killed a white bird up there on her nest,
The down is fluttering from her breast.'
And still it fell through that dusky brightness
On the child crying for the bird of the snow.

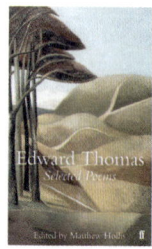

Edward Thomas: Selected Poems (2011)

18 Monday

---

19 Tuesday

---

20 Wednesday

---

21 Thursday

---

22 Friday

---

23 Saturday   24 Sunday

Icefield

A place of ice over ice, of white over white
and beauty in absences. There was a time when the only sound
was the wind calling its ghosts, when the skyline was set

clean as a scar on glass, when your heartbeat slowed
with the cold, when your dreams brought in a white bird
on a white sky and music that could only be heard

from time to time on the other side of night.
Now the horizon's a smudge; now there's a terrible weight
in the air and a stain cut hard and deep in the permafrost.

Breakage and slippage; the rumble of some vast
machine cranking its pistons, of everything on the slide;
and the water rising fast, and the music lost.

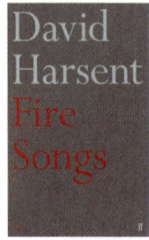

Fire Songs (2014)

25 Monday

---

26 Tuesday

---

27 Wednesday

---

28 Thursday   THANKSGIVING DAY (USA)

---

29 Friday

---

30 Saturday   ST ANDREW'S DAY   1 Sunday

Matthew Francis
The Mabinogi

Poetry

ff

2 Monday   ST ANDREW'S DAY HOLIDAY (SCT)

3 Tuesday

4 Wednesday

5 Thursday

6 Friday

7 Saturday   8 Sunday

A Christmas Poem

At Christmas little children sing and merry bells jingle,
The cold winter air makes our hands and faces tingle
And happy families go to church and cheerily they mingle
And the whole business is unbelievably dreadful, if you're single.

Wendy Cope: Christmas Poems (2017)

9 Monday

10 Tuesday

11 Wednesday

12 Thursday

13 Friday

14 Saturday   15 Sunday

Trance

My mother opens the scullery door
On Christmas Eve, 1954,
to empty the dregs
of the teapot on the snowy flags.
A wind out of Siberia
carries such voices as will carry
through to the kitchen —

Someone mutters a flame from lichen
and eats the red-and-white Fly Agaric
while the others hunker in the dark,
taking it in turn
to drink his mind-expanding urine.
One by one their reindeer
nuzzle in.

My omther slams the door
on her star-cluster of dregs
and packs me off to bed.
At 2 a.m. I will clamber downstairs
to glimpse the red-and-white
up the chimney, my new rocking-horse
as yet unsteady on its legs.

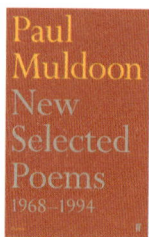

Paul Muldoon: New Selected Poems 1968–1994 (1996)

16 Monday DAY OF RECONCILIATION (ZA)

17 Tuesday

18 Wednesday

19 Thursday

20 Friday

21 Saturday   22 Sunday

Infant Joy

I have no name
I am but two days old. —
What shall I call thee?
I happy am
Joy is my name, —
Sweet joy befall thee!

Pretty joy!
Sweet joy but two days old.
Sweet joy I call thee:
Thou dost smile.
I sing the while
Sweet joy befall thee.

POET TO POET *William Blake: Poems Selected by James Fenton* (2010)

23 Monday   HANUKKAH (FIRST DAY)

24 Tuesday   CHRISTMAS EVE

25 Wednesday   CHRISTMAS DAY (UK, IRL, AUS, NZ, ZA, CAN, USA)

26 Thursday   BOXING DAY (UK, AUS, NZ), ST STEPHEN'S DAY (IRL),
DAY OF GOODWILL (ZA)

27 Friday

28 Saturday   29 Sunday

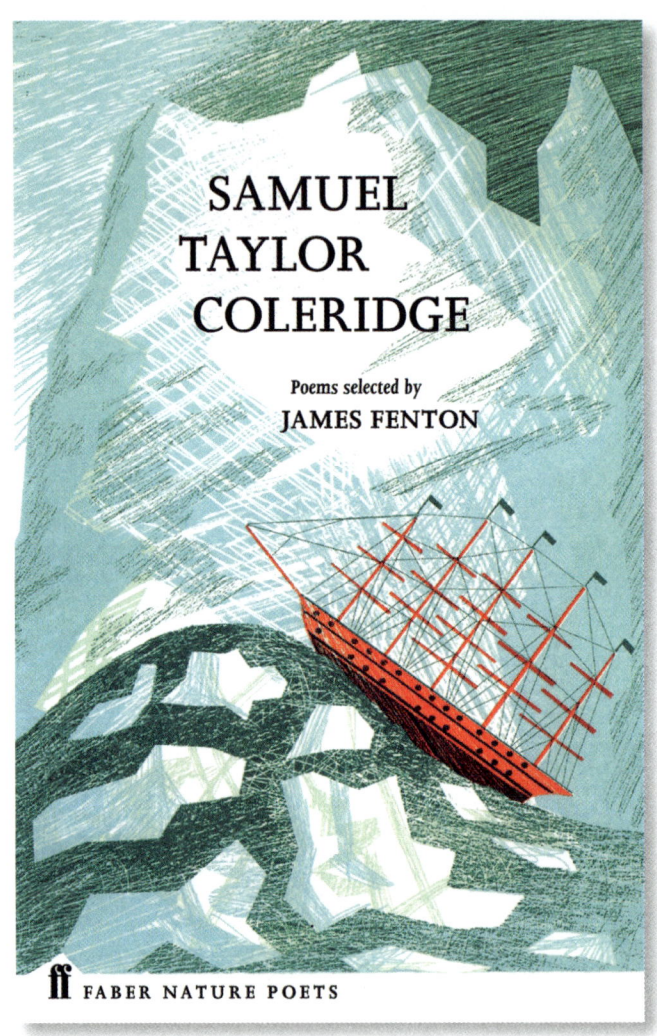

SAMUEL
TAYLOR
COLERIDGE

Poems selected by
JAMES FENTON

ff FABER NATURE POETS

30 Monday

31 Tuesday   NEW YEAR'S EVE

1 Wednesday   NEW YEAR'S DAY (UK, IRL, AUS, ZA, NZ, CAN, USA)

2 Thursday   2ND JANUARY HOLIDAY (SCT), DAY AFTER NEW YEAR'S DAY (NZ)

3 Friday

4 Saturday   5 Sunday

A Brief Chronology of Faber's Poetry Publishing

1925 Geoffrey Faber acquires an interest in The Scientific Press and renames the firm Faber and Gwyer. ¶ The poet/bank clerk T. S. Eliot is recruited. 'What will impress my directors favourably is the sense that in you we have found a man who combines literary gifts with business instincts.' – Geoffrey Faber to T. S. Eliot ¶ Eliot brought with him *The Criterion*, the quarterly periodical he had been editing since 1922. (*The Waste Land* had appeared in its first issue, brilliantly establishing its reputation.) He continued to edit it from the Faber offices until it closed in 1939. Though unprofitable, it was hugely influential, introducing early work by Auden, Empson and Spender, among others, and promoting many notable European writers, including Proust and Valéry. ¶ Publication of T. S. Eliot's *Poems, 1909–1925*, which included *The Waste Land* and a new sequence, *The Hollow Men*. ¶

1927 From 1927 to 1931 Faber publishes a series of illustrated pamphlets known as *The Ariel Poems* containing unpublished poems by an eminent poet (Thomas Hardy, W. B. Yeats, Harold Monro, Edith Sitwell and Edmund Blunden, to name but a few) along with an illustration, usually in colour, by a leading contemporary artist (including Eric Gill, Eric Ravilious, Paul Nash and Graham Sutherland). ¶

1928 Faber and Gwyer announce the *Selected Poems of Ezra Pound*, with an introduction and notes by Eliot. ¶

1929 Geoffrey Faber buys out Lady Gwyer and oversees the birth of the Faber and Faber imprint. Legend has it that Walter de la Mare, the father of Faber director Richard de la Mare, suggested the euphonious repetition: another Faber in the company name 'because you can't have too much of a good thing'. ¶

1930 W. H. Auden becomes a Faber poet with a collection entitled simply *Poems*. ¶ Eliot publishes *Ash Wednesday*. ¶

1933 Stephen Spender becomes a Faber poet with his first collection *Poems*, a companion piece to Auden's 1930 work of the same name. ¶ The first British edition of James Joyce's *Pomes Penyeach* is published. ¶

1935 The American poet Marianne Moore publishes with Faber. 'Miss Moore's poems form part of a small body of durable poetry written in our time.' –T. S. Eliot ¶ Louis MacNeice becomes a Faber poet. 'The most original Irish poet of his generation.' – Faber catalogue 1935 ¶

1936 The hugely influential *Faber Book of Modern Verse* (edited by Michael Roberts) is published. ¶

1937 *In Parenthesis* by David Jones is published. 'This is an epic of war. But it is like no other war-book because for the first time that experience has been reduced to "a shape in words." The impression still remains that this book is one of the most remarkable literary achievements of our time.' – *Times Literary Supplement* ¶ W. H. Auden is awarded the Queen's Gold Medal for Poetry. ¶

1939 T. S. Eliot's *Old Possum's Book of Practical Cats* is published with a book jacket illustrated by the author. Originally called *Pollicle Dogs and Jellicle Cats*, the poems were written for his five godchildren. The eldest of these was Geoffrey Faber's son Tom – himself much later a director of Faber and Faber. ¶

1944 Walter de la Mare's *Peacock Pie* is published with illustrations by Edward Ardizzone. ¶ Philip Larkin's first novel, *A Girl in Winter*, is published. 'A young man with an exceptionally clear sense of what, as a writer, he means to do.' – *Times Literary Supplement* ¶

1948 T. S. Eliot wins the Nobel Prize in Literature. ¶

1949 Ezra Pound's *Pisan Cantos* is published. 'The most incomprehensible passages are often more stimulating than much comprehensibility which passes for poetry today.' – *Times Literary Supplement* ¶

1954 *The Ariel Poems* are revived with a new set of pamphlets by W. H. Auden, Stephen Spender, Louis MacNeice, T. S. Eliot, Walter de la Mare, Cecil Day Lewis and Roy Campbell. The artists include Edward Ardizzone, Edward Bawden, Michael Ayrton and John Piper. ¶

1957 Ted Hughes comes to Faber with *The Hawk in the Rain*. ¶ Siegfried Sassoon receives the Queen's Gold Medal for Poetry. ¶

1959 Robert Lowell's collection *Life Studies* is published. ¶

1960 Saint-John Perse wins the Nobel Prize in Literature. ¶

1961 Geoffrey Faber dies. ¶ Ted Hughes's first collection of children's poems, *Meet My Folks*, is published. ¶

1963 Sylvia Plath's novel *The Bell Jar* is published by Faber in the year of her death. ¶ The Geoffrey Faber Memorial Prize is established as an annual prize awarded in alternating years to a single volume of poetry or fiction by a Commonwealth author under forty. ¶

1964 Philip Larkin's *The Whitsun Weddings* is published. ¶

1965 T. S. Eliot dies. ¶ Sylvia Plath's posthumous collection, *Ariel*, is published. 'Her extraordinary achievement, poised as she was between volatile emotional state and the edge of the precipice.' – Frieda Hughes ¶ Philip Larkin is awarded the Queen's Gold Medal for Poetry. ¶

1966 Seamus Heaney comes to Faber with *Death of a Naturalist*. ¶

1968 Ted Hughes's *The Iron Man* is published. ¶

1971 Stephen Spender is awarded the Queen's Gold Medal for Poetry. ¶

1973 Paul Muldoon comes to Faber with his first collection, *New Weather*. ¶

1974 Ted Hughes receives the Queen's Gold Medal for Poetry. ¶

1977 Tom Paulin comes to Faber with his first collection, *A State of Justice*. ¶ Norman Nicholson receives the Queen's Gold Medal for Poetry. ¶

1980 Czesław Miłosz wins the Nobel Prize in Literature. ¶

1981 *Cats*, the Andrew Lloyd Webber musical based on *Old Possum's Book of Practical Cats*, opens in London. ¶

1984 *Rich*, a collection by Faber's own poetry editor, Craig Raine, is published. 'Puts us in touch with life as unexpectedly and joyfully as early Pasternak.' – John Bayley ¶ Ted Hughes becomes Poet Laureate. ¶

1985 Douglas Dunn's collection *Elegies* is the Whitbread Book of the Year. ¶

1986 Vikram Seth's *The Golden Gate* is published. ¶

1987 Seamus Heaney's *The Haw Lantern* wins the Whitbread Poetry Award. ¶

1988 Derek Walcott is awarded the Queen's Gold Medal for Poetry. ¶

1992 Derek Walcott wins the Nobel Prize in Literature. ¶ Thom Gunn's collection *The Man with the Night Sweats* wins the Forward Poetry Prize for Best Collection, while Simon Armitage's *Kid* wins Best First Collection. ¶

1993 Andrew Motion wins the Whitbread Biography Award for his book on Philip Larkin. ¶ Don Paterson's *Nil Nil* wins the Forward Poetry Prize for Best First Collection. ¶

1994 Paul Muldoon wins the T. S. Eliot Prize for *The Annals of Chile*. ¶ Alice Oswald wins an Eric Gregory Award. ¶

1995 Seamus Heaney wins the Nobel Prize in Literature. ¶

1996 Wisława Szymborska wins the Nobel Prize in Literature. ¶ Seamus Heaney's *The Spirit Level* wins the Whitbread Poetry Award. 'Touched by a sense of wonder.' – Blake Morrison ¶

1997 Don Paterson wins the T. S. Eliot Prize for *God's Gift to Women*. ¶ Lavinia Greenlaw wins the Forward Prize for Best Single Poem for 'A World Where News Travelled Slowly'. ¶ Ted Hughes's *Tales from Ovid* is the Whitbread Book of the Year. 'A breathtaking book.' – John Carey ¶

1998 Ted Hughes wins the Whitbread Book of the Year for the second time running with *Birthday Letters*, which also wins the T. S. Eliot Prize. 'Language like lava, its molten turmoils hardening into jagged shapes.' – John Carey ¶ Ted Hughes is awarded the Order of Merit. ¶ Christopher Logue receives the Wilfred Owen Poetry Award. ¶

1999 Seamus Heaney's *Beowulf* wins the Whitbread Book of the Year Award. '[Heaney is the] one living poet who can rightly claim to be Beowulf's heir.' – *New York Times* ¶ A memorial service for Ted Hughes is held at Westminster Abbey. In his speech Seamus Heaney calls Hughes 'a guardian spirit of the land and language'. ¶ Hugo Williams wins the T. S. Eliot Prize for his collection *Billy's Rain*. ¶ Andrew Motion is appointed Poet Laureate. ¶

2000 Seamus Heaney receives the Wilfred Owen Poetry Award. ¶

2002 Alice Oswald wins the T. S. Eliot Prize for Poetry for her collection *Dart*. ¶

2003 Paul Muldoon is awarded the Pulitzer Prize for Poetry for *Moy Sand and Gravel*. *Landing Light* by Don Paterson wins the Whitbread Poetry Award. ¶

2004 August Kleinzahler receives the International Griffin Poetry Prize for *The Strange Hours Travellers Keep*. ¶ Hugo Williams is awarded the Queen's Gold Medal for Poetry. ¶

2005 David Harsent wins the Forward Prize for Best Collection for *Legion*. ¶ Harold Pinter receives the Wilfred Owen Poetry Award. ¶ Charles Simic receives the International Griffin Poetry Prize for *Selected Poems 1963–2003*. ¶ Nick Laird wins an Eric Gregory Award. ¶

2006 Christopher Logue wins the Whitbread Poetry Award for *Cold Calls*. ¶ The Geoffrey Faber Memorial Prize is awarded to Alice Oswald for *Woods Etc.* ¶ Seamus Heaney wins the T. S. Eliot Prize for *District and Circle*. ¶

2007 Tony Harrison is awarded the Wilfred Owen Poetry Award. ¶ Daljit Nagra wins the Forward Prize for Best First Collection for *Look We Have Coming to Dover!* ¶ James Fenton receives the Queen's Gold Medal for Poetry. ¶

2008 Daljit Nagra wins the South Bank Show / Arts Council Decibel Award. ¶ Mick Imlah's collection *The Lost Leader* wins the Forward Prize for Best Collection. ¶

2009 Carol Ann Duffy becomes Poet Laureate. ¶ Don Paterson's *Rain* wins the Forward Poetry Prize for Best Collection while *The Striped World* by Emma Jones wins the Best First Collection Prize. ¶

2010 *The Song of Lunch* by Christopher Reid is shortlisted for the Ted Hughes Award for New Work in Poetry and he is awarded the Costa Poetry Award for *A Scattering.* ¶ The John Florio Prize for Italian Translation 2010 is awarded to Jamie McKendrick for *The Embrace.* ¶ Derek Walcott wins both the Warwick Prize and the T. S. Eliot Prize for Poetry for his collection *White Egrets.* ¶ *Rain* by Don Paterson is shortlisted for the Saltire Scottish Book of the Year. ¶ Tony Harrison is awarded the Prix Européen de Littérature. ¶ The Keats–Shelley Prize is awarded to Simon Armitage for his poem 'The Present'. ¶ The Forward Prize for Best Collection is awarded to Seamus Heaney for *Human Chain.* ¶ Also shortlisted for the Forward Prize for Best Collection are Lachlan Mackinnon for *Small Hours* and Jo Shapcott for *Of Mutability.* ¶ The Centre for Literacy in Primary Education (CLPE) Poetry Prize is awarded to Carol Ann Duffy for *New and Collected Poems for Children.* ¶ Alice Oswald wins the Ted Hughes Award for New Work in Poetry for *Weeds and Wild Flowers.* ¶ *The Striped World* by Emma Jones is shortlisted for the Adelaide Festival Poetry Award. ¶ The Queen's Gold Medal for Poetry is awarded to Don Paterson. ¶

2011 *Of Mutability* by Jo Shapcott is the Costa Book of the Year. ¶ *Human Chain* by Seamus Heaney and *Maggot* by Paul Muldoon are both shortlisted for the *Irish Times* Poetry Now Award. ¶ *Night* by David Harsent is shortlisted for the Forward Prize for Best Collection. ¶ 'Bees' by Jo Shapcott is shortlisted for the Forward Prize for Best Single Poem. ¶ A new digital edition of T. S. Eliot's *The Waste Land* for iPad is launched, bringing to life one of the most revolutionary poems of the last hundred years, illuminated by a wealth of interactive features. ¶ The Queen's Gold Medal for Poetry is awarded to Jo Shapcott. ¶ At Westminster Abbey a memorial is dedicated to Ted Hughes in Poets' Corner. ¶

2012 *The Death of King Arthur* by Simon Armitage is shortlisted for the T. S. Eliot Prize. ¶ *The World's Two Smallest Humans* by Julia Copus is shortlisted for the T. S. Eliot Prize and the Costa Poetry Award. ¶ David Harsent's collection *Night* wins the International Griffin Poetry Prize. ¶ *81 Austerities* by Sam Riviere wins the Felix Dennis Prize for Best First Collection, one of the Forward Prizes for Poetry. ¶ *Farmers Cross* by Bernard O'Donoghue is shortlisted for the *Irish Times* Poetry Now Award. ¶

2013 The Forward Prize for Best First Collection is awarded to Emily Berry for *Dear Boy.* ¶ Hugo Williams is shortlisted for the Forward Prize for Best Single

Poem for 'From the Dialysis Ward'. ¶ Alice Oswald is awarded the Warwick Prize for Writing for her collection *Memorial*, which also wins the Poetry Society's Corneliu M. Popescu Prize for poetry in translation. ¶ The Queen's Gold Medal for Poetry is awarded to Douglas Dunn. ¶ The shortlist for the T. S. Eliot Prize includes Daljit Nagra for *The Ramayana: A Retelling* and Maurice Riordan for *The Water Stealer*. ¶ *Pink Mist* by Owen Sheers wins the Hay Festival Medal for Poetry. ¶ In his eulogy for Seamus Heaney, Paul Muldoon says, 'We remember the beauty of Seamus Heaney – as a bard, and in his being.' In November the first official tribute evenings to Heaney are held at Harvard, then in New York, followed by events at the Royal Festival Hall in London, the Waterfront Hall, Belfast, and the Sheldonian, Oxford. ¶

2014 Maurice Riordan is shortlisted for the Pigott Poetry Prize for *The Water Stealer*. ¶ Hugo Williams is shortlisted for the Forward Prize for Best Collection for *I Knew the Bride*. ¶ Daljit Nagra is awarded the Society of Authors Travelling Scholarship. ¶ Nick Laird's *Go Giants* is shortlisted for the *Irish Times* Poetry Now Award. ¶ Emily Berry, Emma Jones and Daljit Nagra are announced as three of the Poetry Book Society's Next Generation Poets 2014. ¶ *Pink Mist* by Owen Sheers is named the Wales Book of the Year after winning the poetry category. ¶

2015 *Fire Songs* by David Harsent is awarded the T. S. Eliot Prize for Poetry. ¶ Alice Oswald wins the Ted Hughes Award for New Work for *Tithonus*, a poem and performance commissioned by London's Southbank Centre. ¶ *One Thousand Things Worth Knowing* by Paul Muldoon wins the Pigott Poetry Prize. ¶ Don Paterson is awarded the Neustadt International Prize for Literature. ¶ *Terror* by Toby Martinez de las Rivas is shortlisted for the Seamus Heaney Centre for Poetry's Prize for First Full Collection. ¶ Paul Muldoon's *One Thousand Things Worth Knowing* is shortlisted for the Forward Prize for Best Collection. ¶ James Fenton is awarded the Pen Pinter Prize. ¶ *40 Sonnets* by Don Paterson wins the Costa Poetry Award, and is short-listed for the T. S. Eliot Prize. ¶

2016 Don Paterson is shortlisted for the International Griffin Poetry Prize. ¶ *40 Sonnets* by Don Paterson is short-listed for the Saltire Society Literary Awards. ¶ *The Seasons of Cullen Church* by Bernard O'Donoghue is shortlisted for the T. S. Eliot Prize. ¶ Jack Underwood receives a Somerset Maugham Award. ¶ An excerpt from *Salt* by David Harsent is shortlisted for the Forward Prize for Best Single Poem. ¶

2017 *The Unaccompanied* by Simon Armitage, *Stranger, Baby* by Emily Berry and *The Noise of a Fly* by Douglas Dunn all receive Recommendations from the Poetry Book Society. They also give a Special Commendation to

Selected Poems of Thom Gunn, edited by Clive Wilmer. ¶ Simon Armitage receives the PEN Award for Poetry in Translation for *Pearl* ¶ Bernard O'Donoghue's collection *The Seasons of Cullen Church* is shortlisted for the Pigott Poetry Prize. ¶ Emily Berry's collection *Stranger, Baby* is shortlisted for the Forward Prize for Best Collection. ¶ Sam Riviere's collection *Kim Kardashian's Marriage* is shortlisted for the Ledbury Poetry Prize. ¶ Douglas Dunn's collection *The Noise of a Fly* is shortlisted for the T. S. Eliot Prize. ¶

Acknowledgements

Poetry

All poetry reprinted by permission of Faber & Faber alone unless otherwise stated.

'The Crotchet' taken from *Curiosities* © Christopher Reid 2015. Reproduced by permission of the author c/o Rogers, Coleridge & White Ltd., 20 Powis Mews, London, W11 1JN ¶ 'Roe-deer' taken from *Collected Poems* © The Estate of Ted Hughes. Reprinted by permission of Faber & Faber Ltd., and Farrar, Straus & Giroux, LLC., New York ¶ 'The Slim Man' taken from *Faber New Poets 9* © Rachael Allen. Reprinted by permission of Faber & Faber Ltd ¶ 'The Net Menders' taken from *Collected Poems* © The Estate of Sylvia Plath. Reprinted by permission of Faber & Faber Ltd, and HarperCollins Publishers, New York ¶ 'The Unaccompanied' taken from *The Unaccompanied* © Simon Armitage. Reprinted by permission of Faber & Faber Ltd, and David Godwin Associates Ltd ¶ 'A double sorrow' taken from *A Double Sorrow* © Lavinia Greenlaw. Reprinted by permission of Faber & Faber Ltd, and W. W. Norton & Company, Inc. ¶ 'Prelude to the Afternoon of a Faun' taken from *House of Lords and Commons* © Ishion Hutchinson. Reprinted by permission of Faber & Faber Ltd, and Farrar, Straus & Giroux, LLC., New York ¶ 'Self-Portrait on The Levels' taken from *Faber New Poets 2* © Toby Martinez de las Rivas. Reprinted by permission of Faber & Faber Ltd ¶ 'Cut Grass' taken from *The Complete Poems* © The Estate of Philip Larkin. Reprinted by permission of Faber & Faber Ltd, and Farrar, Straus & Giroux, LLC., New York ¶ 'le jardin secret' taken from *Soho* © Richard Scott. Reprinted by permission

Picture credits

PARK 6282.

May 28 '25

21, LADBROKE GROVE,
W. 11.

My dear Eliot

I am v. glad to have 'The Waste
Land'. You won't think it unkind of
me to say that I am excitedly groping
in it. You _are_ obscure, you know!
with an obscurity compared to which
Meredith at his most bewildering [& he
can baffle, too] is the purest ray
serene. I wonder if you realize how
difficult you are? & alternatively I
wonder if I am specially stupid. Is
it that you are using a language of
which I have learnt only the vocabulary
but not the syntax? — I haven't

yet got the key to your poetry;
I say frankly. You try the stranger
a little high: only those who have trod
the same labyrinth as yourself can
follow the clue. The others must put
too much detective-work into their reading,
to lose the sense of the chase in the
understanding of the thing captured
— I, mean, one asks oneself if it
isn't really something quite other than
one had at first thought.

Please understand me — this is <u>not</u>
Criticism. I am profoundly sensible,
in reading The Waste Land, as I
was in reading your 3-fold "Eyes"
poem in the Criterion, of a meaning
not the less truly there because I

PARK 6282.

21, LADBROKE GROVE,
W. 11.

can only grasp it fragmentarily — of
astounding vivid glimpses of now of
the pit beneath the human mind,
& now of beauties seen & painted in
the sharp startling precision of phrase
of which, at your best, you are master.

    There the eyes are

        Sunlight on a broken column

                                              — —.

How thin my own stuff must seem
to you!

    Well, I write like this, tho' it may be
an odd way of thanking you for a gift,
because I will not pretend to understand
what I don't understand; & I suspect
that a good many people have praised

The *Waste Land* who hadn't the faintest atom of an idea what it was all about !! You have the pull on them – but here on me. I daresay posterity will wonder that anybody could have found you obscure – or puzzle at people's obtuseness over *Prufrock* &c.

Having said that, you won't suspect me of flattering you, when I reiterate that you *do* impress, & impress with a sense of a new way of seeing & relating things, which will be understood all in good time; & meanwhile gives bright unforgettable landing-places.

I wonder if I dare send you all this !

———

NOTES

Faber
Members

In 2019, Faber & Faber marks its 90th anniversary as one of the world's most prestigious publishing houses.

From the 1920s to the present day, Faber has always published the most distinctive literature in the language.

Join us in celebrating our anniversary by signing up to our Members programme in 2019. As a Faber Member you will receive updates about our books and our renowned list of authors as well as hidden gems from the Faber archive. You will also have access to our special events, exclusive promotions, and customer discounts throughout the anniversary year and into the future.

Faber Members: bringing you closer to the books you love. Visit www.fabermembers.com for more details.